BIBLE DETECTIVE
JOHN
Puzzle Book

Written by Ros Woodman
Illustrated by Ron Wheeler

Wordsearch Puzzles designed by Chris Woodman
Cover Design by Alister MacInnes
Illustration Ron Wheeler
Printed and bound by Bell and Bain, Glasgow
Published by Christian Focus Publications
Geanies House, Fearn, Tain, Ross-shire, IV20 1TW, Scotland, UK.
www.christianfocus.com email: info@christianfocus.com

© copyright 2002 Christian Focus Publications
Reprinted 2006
ISBN: 1-85792-759-1, 978-1-85792-759-7

Hello, We're Harry and Jess! We're *The Bible Detectives Team* and we're on an adventure through John's Gospel. We're going to find out more about Jesus. Come with us and together with Click, we'll discover lots about God and his word. What do you have for us now Click?

JOHN

Author of John's Gospel
Son of Zebedee
Brother of James

A disciple of Jesus, said to be 'the one whom Jesus loved.'

Purpose in writing the Gospel

So that you may believe that Jesus is the Messiah the Son of God and that believing in him you will have life.   John 20: 31.

It's an info file about John - the man who wrote John's gospel!

Gospel

Gospel is another word for Good News. Some books of the New Testament are called Gospels - Matthew, Mark, Luke and John. It also describes the good news that we read in the Bible, which is - Jesus died to save us from our sins.

The Bible

This is God's book. He used people to do the physical writing. Prophets, men of God, the disciples - they all wrote down or told other people what it was that God said to them. There are two sections. The Old Testament happened before Jesus was born and The New Testament is about Jesus' life, death and resurrection. It is also about what his followers did after he went back to heaven. The Old Testament is made up of 39 separate books. The New Testament is made up of 27 books. Each Bible book is divided up into smaller sections called chapters. Each chapter is divided up into smaller parts called verses. Books, chapters and verses actually make it easier to find things in the Bible. When this investigation is finished you will remember that the stories discovered are in the Book of John. John is the fourth book of the New Testament. The Bible is God's word to us. The gospels are full of true life stories of people that Jesus met. We will investigate some of them in this book... it's amazing to realise that these things really happened and that every word from God is true!

THE FIRST DISCIPLES

After Jesus had been baptised, he began to gather a group of followers. They were called disciples - and here's what happened ....

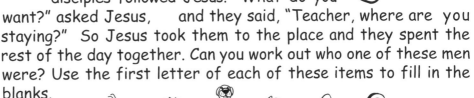

John the Baptist was standing with two of his disciples when Jesus walked past. "Look, this is the Lamb of God," said John, and the two disciples followed Jesus. "What do you want?" asked Jesus, and they said, "Teacher, where are you staying?" So Jesus took them to the place and they spent the rest of the day together. Can you work out who one of these men were? Use the first letter of each of these items to fill in the blanks.

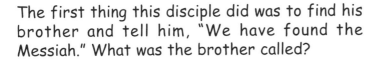

__ __ __ __ __ __

The first thing this disciple did was to find his brother and tell him, "We have found the Messiah." What was the brother called?

__ __ __ __ __

The Scriptures said that a Messiah would come one day, and the Jews had been waiting for him to come. When Jesus saw this next man, he told him his name but then he said that he would also be called - Cephas. Which meant rock. What was his name?

__ __ __ __ __

The next day, Jesus went to Galilee and met another man. "Come, be my disciple," he said, and the man followed. What was his name?

__ __ __ __ __ __ __

This disciple went to look for another man. He said, "We have found the person that Moses and the prophets wrote about. He is Jesus of Nazareth, the son of Joseph. Who was he talking to?

__ __ __ __ __ __ __ __ __ __

After talking with Jesus, Nathanael was amazed and declared, "Teacher, you are the Son of God, the King of Israel."

3

THE WEDDING AT CANA

Jesus performed his first miracle at a wedding. We've been finding out all about it. Click's here to help.

Jesus' mother was a guest at a wedding in the village of Cana in Galilee. Jesus and his disciples were also invited, and part way through there was a problem.

"Jesus", said Mary, his mother, "they have run out of wine." Jesus replied, "How does that concern us? My time hasn't come yet." But Mary turned to the servants and said, "Do whatever he says."

There were six stone water pots there. They were used for Jewish ceremonial washing and held 75-115 litres each.
"Fill them with water," said Jesus.
When the jars had been filled, Jesus told them to take some out and give it to the master of the banquet. The water had turned into wine.

The master did not know what had happened, although the servants did. He called the bridegroom over and said, "Usually a host serves the best wine first. Then, when everyone is full and doesn't care, he brings out the cheaper wine.
But you have kept the best till now."

And after this, the disciples put their faith in Jesus.

Can you find 5 bunches of grapes hidden in the picture?

Can you find 6 spiders in the first picture and seven goblets in the second picture?

JESUS CLEARS THE TEMPLE

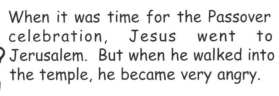

When it was time for the Passover celebration, Jesus went to Jerusalem. But when he walked into the temple, he became very angry.

John 2: 13-25

HOLY BIBLE

Instead of a place of prayer, it was a noisy market. Merchants sold cattle, sheep and doves, and moneychangers traded busily. Can you imagine the hustle and bustle and the smell of dung? Jesus then made a whip from some ropes and chased them all out of the temple. He turned over the tables of the money changers. Money was scattered all over the floor. He said to the people selling doves, "Get these things out of here. Don't turn my Father's house into a market place!" The disciples remembered a prophecy about Jesus written in the scriptures long before this moment. Can you work it out? Ignore all the X's

_ _ _ _   _ _ _

_ _ _ _   _ _ _ _ _

_ _ _ _ _ _ _ _

_ _.   Psalm 69:9

The Jewish leaders were not happy. "Who gave you authority to do this?" they said. "Show us a miraculous sign to prove that you have it." Jesus said,

"Destroy this temple and I will raise it again in three days." "It's taken 46 years to build this temple, and you are going to raise it in three days?" they said. Answer the questions below and the vertical column will reveal what Jesus meant by "this temple."

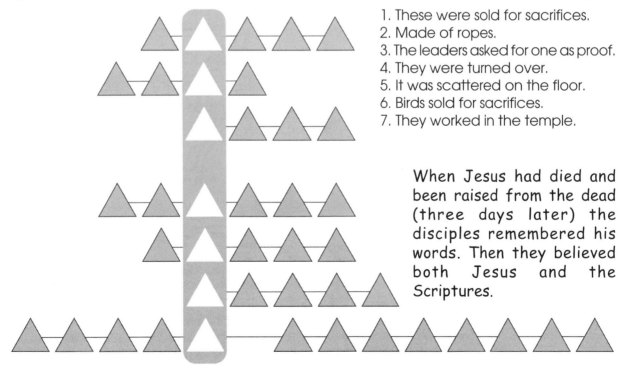

1. These were sold for sacrifices.
2. Made of ropes.
3. The leaders asked for one as proof.
4. They were turned over.
5. It was scattered on the floor.
6. Birds sold for sacrifices.
7. They worked in the temple.

When Jesus had died and been raised from the dead (three days later) the disciples remembered his words. Then they believed both Jesus and the Scriptures.

JESUS TEACHES NICODEMUS

 A man named Nicodemus came to see Jesus after dark one night. He was a religious leader on the Jewish ruling council.

 Teacher, we know that God has sent you to teach us. We have proof that God is with you when we see your miraculous signs.

Jesus replied:

"I tell you the truth. Unless you are born again you can never see the Kingdom of God." Nicodemus was very puzzled by this reply.

What do you mean? How can an old man go back into his mother's womb and be born again?

Jesus said: The truth is, no-one can enter the Kingdom of God without being born of water and the Spirit.

Humans can only reproduce human life but the Holy Spirit gives new life from heaven. Don't be surprised when I say you must be born again. Just as you hear the wind but can't tell here it's coming from or where it goes, so you can't explain how people are born of the Spirit.

John 3:1-21

Nicodemus still didn't understand, so Jesus carried on.

You are a respected teacher but you don't understand? If you don't believe when I tell you about earthly things, how can you believe if I tell you what goes on in heaven.

I am the only one who has come to earth and will go back to heaven. And just as Moses lifted up a bronze snake on a pole in the desert, so I must be lifted up on a pole. Then everyone who believes in me will have eternal life.

Click has found the Bible reference for you to find this story about Moses. It's in the Old Testament... show us where it is Click.

Numbers 21:1-9

When Jesus told the people about this story he was actually telling them about something else. He was talking about the way he was going to die. Why was Jesus talking about death? And why did Jesus come to the world in the first place? Jesus spoke some very important words to Nicodemus. Fill in the missing vowels to find out what Jesus said and find out about why Jesus came.

F_r G_d s_ l_v_d th_ w_rld th_t h_ g_v_

h_s _nly S_n s_ th_t _v_ry_n_ wh_

b_l_ _v_s _n h_m w_ll n_t p_r_sh b_t

h_v_ _t_rn_l l_f_. G_d d_d n_t s_nd h_s

s_n _nt_ th_ w_rld t_ c_nd_mn _t

b_t t_ s_v_ _t. **John 3:16**

Jesus also spoke these words of wisdom.

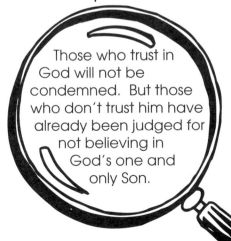

Those who trust in God will not be condemned. But those who don't trust him have already been judged for not believing in God's one and only Son.

Their judgement is based on this. Light from heaven came into the world. But they loved darkness more than light because their actions were evil.

They hate the light because they want to sin in darkness. They stay away from the light because they don't want their sins to be seen. They don't want to be punished.

Fill in the missing vowels to find out what else Jesus said.

Th_s_   wh_   d_   wh_t   _s   r_ght   c_m_

t_   th_   L_ght   gl_dly,   s_   _v_ry_n_   c_n   s__

th_t   th_y   _r_   d__ng   wh_t   G_d   w_nts.

Crossword

Across

1. Some people fear these will be exposed.
5 & 16. The promise for those who believe in Jesus (2 words).
7. You must be born of this and the Spirit
9. To loosen or undo.
10. He lifted up a snake.
12. A question you might ask beginning with the letter H.
14. Not women.
16. See 5 across.
18. Those who do this hate the light.
19. Some feel this way towards the light.
20. The Son of Man came to this planet.
21. How many sons did God have?

Down

2. To look at.
3. Not lies.
4. Jesus came into the world to do this.
6. There is no judgement for those who put this in Jesus.
8. One of the five senses.
11. How can a man be born again when he is this?
12. Jesus was going to return there.
13. God loved it so much that he sent his son.
15. Nicodemus came at this time.
17. The Son of Man would be lifted up on it.

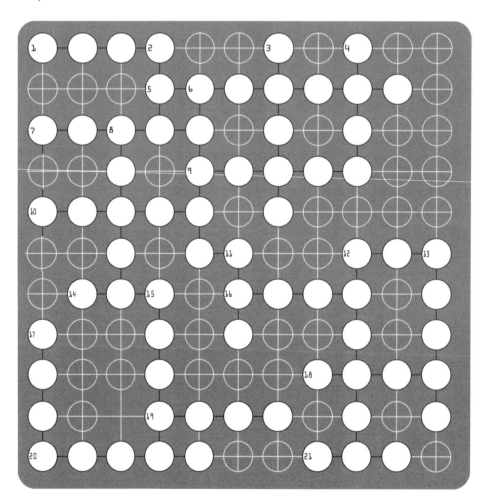

JOHN THE BAPTIST EXALTS JESUS

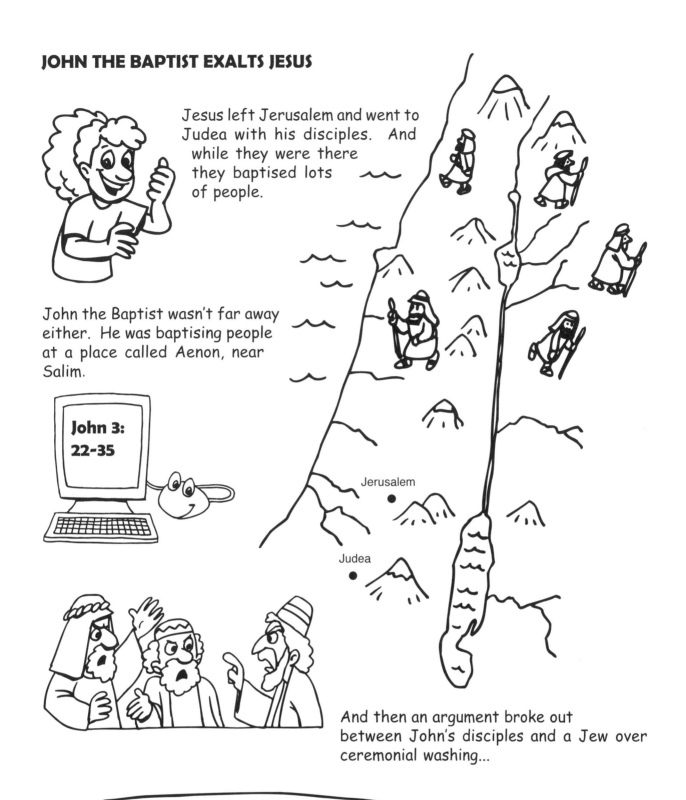

Jesus left Jerusalem and went to Judea with his disciples. And while they were there they baptised lots of people.

John the Baptist wasn't far away either. He was baptising people at a place called Aenon, near Salim.

John 3: 22-35

Jerusalem

Judea

And then an argument broke out between John's disciples and a Jew over ceremonial washing...

Teacher, that man on the other side of the Jordan river - the one you said was the Messiah. Well, he is baptising people too. And everyone is going over there instead of coming to us.

And John said

It is God who chooses each person's work. I'm not the Messiah. I'm here to prepare the way for him.

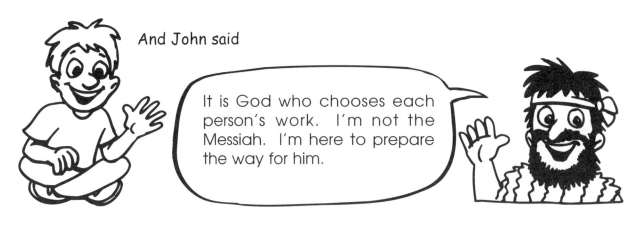

John explained that he was like a friend of a bridegroom. He was filled with joy at Jesus' success. Can you match the pictures to find out what he said.

must become   and I   He must   and greater   and less   greater   less   become

John explained that Jesus was greater than anyone. John could only understand the things of earth, but Jesus was from heaven. Look at the words inside the balloons all of these were said by John the Baptist. Work out the missing word in the top/middle balloon by taking the initial letter of all the other objects on the next page and inserting them in the spaces.

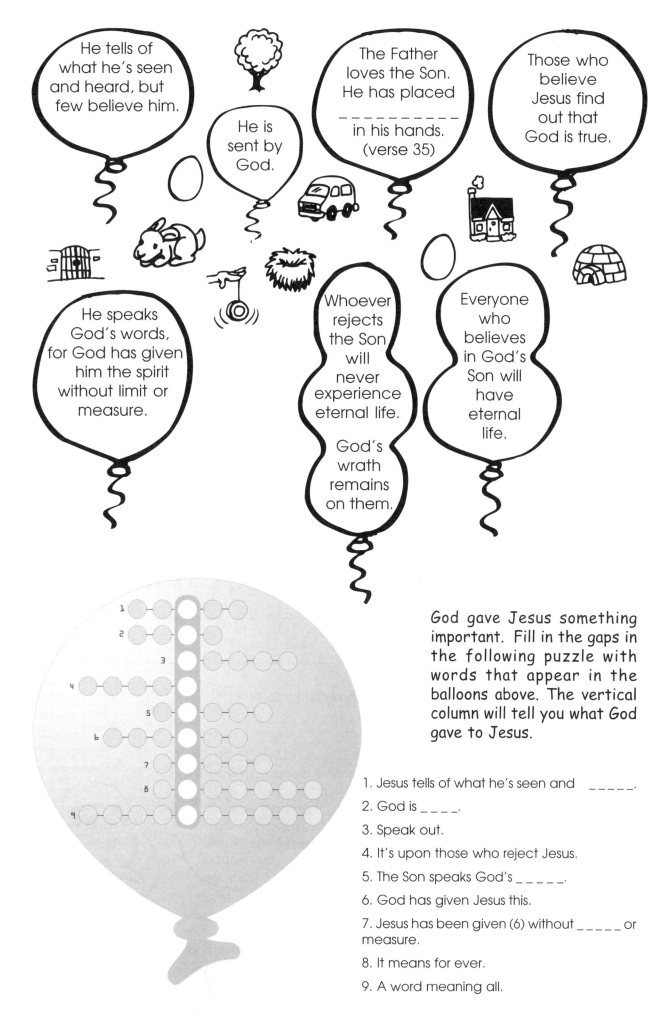

He tells of what he's seen and heard, but few believe him.

He is sent by God.

The Father loves the Son. He has placed _ _ _ _ _ _ _ _ _ in his hands. (verse 35)

Those who believe Jesus find out that God is true.

He speaks God's words, for God has given him the spirit without limit or measure.

Whoever rejects the Son will never experience eternal life. God's wrath remains on them.

Everyone who believes in God's Son will have eternal life.

God gave Jesus something important. Fill in the gaps in the following puzzle with words that appear in the balloons above. The vertical column will tell you what God gave to Jesus.

1. Jesus tells of what he's seen and _ _ _ _ _.
2. God is _ _ _ _.
3. Speak out.
4. It's upon those who reject Jesus.
5. The Son speaks God's _ _ _ _ _.
6. God has given Jesus this.
7. Jesus has been given (6) without _ _ _ _ _ or measure.
8. It means for ever.
9. A word meaning all.

11

JESUS AND THE SAMARITAN WOMAN

John 4:1-38

Jesus was always surprising his disciples.

Yes. Like in this story below when he talked to a Samaritan woman. Can you find the story, Click?

Jesus and the disciples came to a village called Sychar in Samaria. It was noon, and Jesus sat down by a well to rest. He was tired after a   long walk. Jesus was alone because the disciples had gone into the village to buy food. Soon, a Samaritan woman came to draw water, and Jesus said to her, "Please, give me a drink."

The woman was surprised because Jews refuse to have anything to do with Samaritans, and women were looked down upon. She said to Jesus, "Why are you asking me for a drink?"

She obviously didn't know who Jesus was. Can you work out Jesus' reply?

Put into order

→

Start

Answer: _____

_____ John 4:10

Well, as you can guess, the woman was puzzled.

"But Sir, the well is very deep and you don't have a rope or bucket. And where would you get this living water? Are you greater than our ancestor Jacob who gave us this well? How can you offer better water?"

Jesus said: Everyone who drinks water will become thirsty again. But the water I give them takes away thirst completely. It becomes a spring of water, giving them eternal life.

This is all very puzzling, so we've found out more.

Yes, Jesus was using picture language to explain what happens when you put your trust in him. The Holy Spirit comes to live in you and you are filled with joy because you know that you will live for ever with Jesus. Let's carry on.

Jesus kept talking to the woman. He told her that he knew she's had five husbands, and that he knew she was not married to the man she was living with now. Can you imagine how amazed she felt? But more was about to happen. The woman said to Jesus,

So Jesus told her

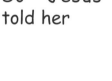

I know that the Messiah, the Christ is coming. When he does he will explain everything.

I am the Messiah.

And then the disciples came back. But what happened next Harry?

Well Jess, the woman ran back to the village and told everyone,

Come and meet a man who told me everything I ever did! Can this be the Messiah.

People came streaming out of the village, and many people believed in Jesus because of what the woman had said. They begged Jesus to stay, so he remained there for 2 days. Here's what they said afterwards - Study the key well before you start - one or two symbols look very similar.

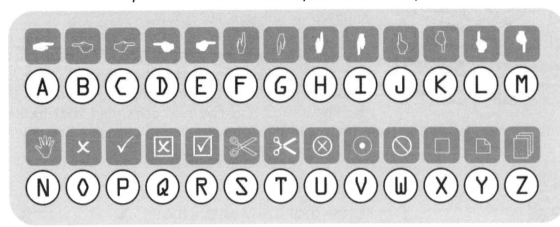

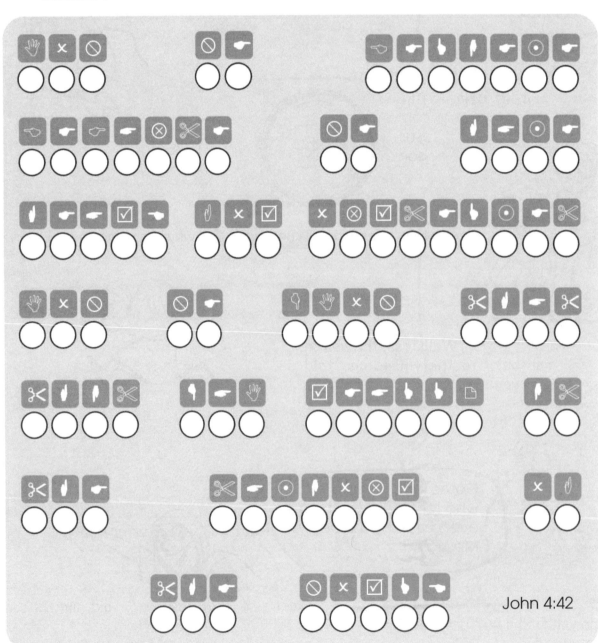

John 4:42

JESUS HEALS AN OFFICIAL'S SON

John 4: 43-53

Hi Detectives, Harry and I are on the move again. Jesus was always on the move. After staying in Samaria, he went on to Galilee where he was warmly welcomed. The people here had seen all the miraculous signs he'd performed at the Passover in Jerusalem.

Click has emailed us about what happened in a place called Capernaum. There's a picture too ... can you spot the butterfly? It's very tiny!

There was a royal official in Capernaum whose son was dying. He went to Jesus and begged him to heal his son.

Jesus said, "Must I do miraculous signs and miracles before you believe in me?" But the man pleaded with him.

Then Jesus told the man to go, and that his son would live.

The man believed Jesus and left. While he was on the way, his servants came and told him that his son was alive and well.

The man asked the servants at what time had his son begun to get better. They told him that it was at the seventh hour.

Can you find a butterfly in this picture too?

And guess what? He realised that it was the exact time that Jesus had told him his son would live! So the official and his whole household believed in Jesus.

THE HEALING AT THE POOL

Once again Jesus was on the move, this time to Jerusalem to celebrate one of the Jewish holy days.

Can you spot the three differences between them?

In the city, near the Sheep Gate was the pool of Bethesda, with 5 covered porches. Lots of people with different sicknesses came here - the blind, the lame and the paralysed. They believed that there was healing for the first person to get into the pool when the water stirred. A man had been lying there who had been sick for 38 years. And when Jesus learned of this, he asked, "Do you want to get well?"

The man said, "I can't, Sir. There is no-one to help me get into the pool when the water is stirred, and when I'm trying to get in, someone always gets there before me." Jesus said, "Get up. Pick up your mat and walk." The man was cured at once. He rolled up his mat and walked!

But trouble was afoot. You see, Jesus had healed the man on the Sabbath, and it was forbidden to carry a mat on that day.

"Who did this?" asked the Jews. You'd think they'd be happy that someone had been healed, wouldn't you Harry. But the man couldn't help them because Jesus had disappeared into the crowd.

Later on, Jesus found the man in the temple and he said, "You are well now. So stop sinning or something worse might happen to you." Then the man went away and told the Jews that it was Jesus who had made him well.

JESUS CLAIMS TO BE THE SON OF GOD

By now, Jess, the Jewish leaders really disliked Jesus and they wanted to kill him. It wasn't just because he broke Jewish rules by healing on the Sabbath. It was also because he claimed to be the Son of God.

You know, Harry, Jesus had something very important to say, and he wasn't going to let them stop him yet. Can you fit the jigsaw pieces together to work out what he said. You can use the guide at the bottom of the page to help.

Jesus said, I assure you that...

Those who listen to my

condemned for their sins

already passed

from death into life

in God who sent me

They will never be

have eternal life

but they have

message and believe

Answer:_____

_____

And Jesus scolded the Jews. Here are some of the things he said (use the code to fill in the gaps.)

KEY

A ✳	C ♥	D ●	E ▲	F ◖	G ◆
H ◉	I ♡	L ○	M △	N ▢	O ◇
P ▽	R ◼	S ▯	T ◗	U ■	Y ▼

1

You think that the **SCRIPTURES**

give you eternal life so you

study them. But the **SCRIPTURES**

point to me! Yet you **REFUSE** to

come to me so that I can give

you **ETERNAL** **LIFE**

2

I have come to you

representing my **FATHER**

But you do not **ACCEPT**

me. But you will accept

someone else who comes in

his **NAME**

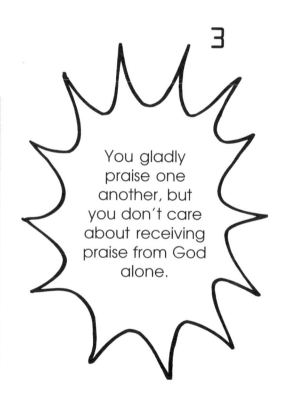

3

You gladly praise one another, but you don't care about receiving praise from God alone.

18

JESUS FEEDS THE FIVE THOUSAND

Harry, can you imagine how it must feel to be followed by crowds of people all the time? Jesus knew! People saw the signs and wonders he performed and they followed him everywhere. Take this day, for example ...

One day, Jesus crossed the sea of Galilee and went up on to a mountainside with his disciples and sat down. But when Jesus looked up, he saw a huge crowd coming.

Match up the broken pieces of bread to see what he said to Philip.

Start

Where people

buy these bread we for shall

Answer : _____

The Bible says that Jesus had already decided what he would do, but he had asked Philip to test him. Follow the lines to see what Philip said.

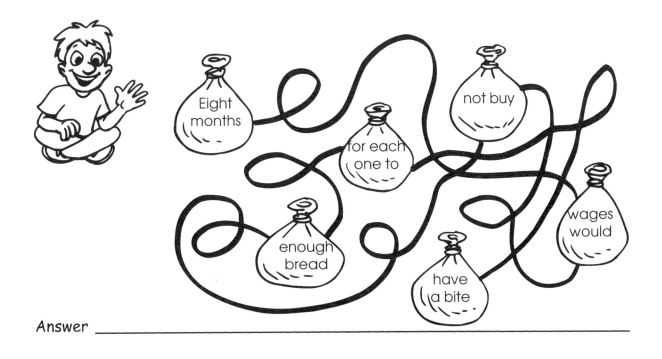

Eight months   for each one to   not buy   enough bread   have a bite   wages would

Answer _____

_____

Then Simon-Peter's brother Andrew spoke up.

There's a boy here with 5 barley loaves and 2 fish. But that's not much good for this huge crowd.

But Jesus had other plans. Everyone had to sit down - about 5000 people. Then Jesus took the loaves, gave thanks to God and passed them round. He did the same with the fish. Afterwards, they gathered up the left-overs.

Can you finish the phrases below and fill in the squares. The diagonal squares will spell out how many baskets were left.

1. _ _ _ _ overs
2. _ _ _ fish
3. _ _ _ _ _ months
4. Sea of _ _ _ _ _ _ _
5. Barley _ _ _ _ _ _
6. Simon _ _ _ _ _

And do you know, Jess? When the people saw this miraculous sign, this is what they said

S _ R_LY   H_ _S   TH_   PR_PH_T   W_   H_V_   B_ _ N   _XP_CT_NG!

Fill in the missing vowels.

They were ready to take him by force and make him king. So Jesus went higher into the hills to be alone.

JESUS WALKS ON WATER

That evening, Jess, the disciples went down to the shore to wait for Jesus.

Can you find six fish?

John 6: 16-21

Darkness fell, so they decided to get into their boat and go across the lake to Capernaum.

A storm blew up as they rowed and the sea got very rough.

Can you find a seagull sheltering from the storm?

Then an amazing thing happened which terrified the disciples. They saw Jesus walking on the water towards them.

What other animal has now joined the seagull?

Jesus called to them, "I am here. Don't be afraid." They were so glad to see him!! He climbed into the boat and immediately, the boat reached their destination.

JESUS THE BREAD OF LIFE

Many people came to find Jesus, and here are some of the things he said to them. Come on Bible Detectives, can you fill in the gaps?

John 6: 25-59

I am the _ _ _ _ _   _ _   _ _ _ _.

Whoever comes to me will never

be _ _ _ _ _ _ again. Whoever

believes in me will never be _ _ _ _ _ _ _.

Those whom the

_ _ _ _ _ _ has given me

will come to me, and I will _ _ _ _ _ drive them away.

It's my Father's will that _ _ _ _ _ _ _ _ who

sees his son and _ _ _ _ _ _ _ _ in him shall

have eternal life.

Some of Jesus' followers found it too hard to accept his teaching and some stopped following him. Jesus asked his disciples if they wanted to leave too. What did Simon-Peter say? Use Click's keyboard to work out the code. Each number has a letter - so the first two letters are L and O.

Q	W	E	R	T	Y	U	I	O	P
1	2	3	4	5	6	7	8	9	10

A	S	D	F	G	H	J	K	L
11	12	13	14	15	16	17	18	19

Z	X	C	V	B	N	M	,	.
20	21	22	23	24	25	26	27	28

19,9,4,13   5,9   2,16,9,26

_ _ _ _   _ _   _ _ _ _

2,9,7,19,13   2,3   15,9

_ _ _ _ _   _ _   _ _ ?

9,25,19,6   6,9,7

_ _ _ _   _ _ _

16,11,23,3   5,16,3   2,9,4,13,12   5,16,11,5   15,8,23,3   3,5,3,4,25,11,19

_ _ _ _   _ _ _   _ _ _ _ _   _ _ _ _   _ _ _ _   _ _ _ _ _ _ _

19,8,14,3.   2,3   24,3,19,8,3,23,3   5,16,3,26   11,25,13   2,3   18,25,9,2

_ _ _ _ .   _ _   _ _ _ _ _ _ _   _ _ _ _   _ _ _   _ _   _ _ _ _

6,9,7   11,4,3   5,16,3   16,9,19,6   9,25,3   9,14   15,9,13.

_ _ _   _ _ _   _ _ _   _ _ _ _   _ _ _   _ _   _ _ _ .

22

JESUS AND HIS BROTHERS

John 7:1-9

Jess, did you know that Jesus had brothers? Well, they didn't believe in him either. When it was time for the Jewish Festival of Shelters, they urged him to go to Judea for the celebration. But Jesus wanted to stay away because the Jewish leaders were plotting his death. Let's find out, Harry, what Jesus' brothers said to him. Click's going to email us with the Bible reference too. Detectives - before you do the following puzzles why not look up the reference in your own Bible if you have one and read this story there!

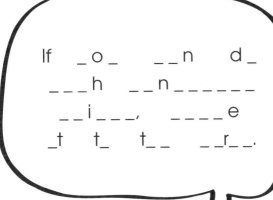

If _ o _   _ _ n   d _
_ _ _ h   _ _ n _ _ _ _ _
_ _ i _ _ _ ,   _ _ _ _ e
_ t   t _   t _ _   _ _ r _ _ .

To work out what these people said to Jesus fill in the gaps with these words.

You can't become a public figure by acting in secret.

you   to   prove   such
the   do   it   can
wonderful   things   world

Jesus wasn't going to be pushed into doing anything, and he told his brothers that it wasn't the right time for him to go. He said, "You can go at any time and it won't make a difference." What else did he say to them?

_ h _ _
_ _ l _

_ _ a _ '
_ _ t

y _ _

b _ _ i _

_ _ _ _ s
_ e

_ _ c _ _ _ _
_

_ _ _ u _ _
_ t o _

_ i _
d
_ _ _ i _

but it

The World

hates me

because I

sin and evil.

you,

accuse it of

can't hate

24

JESUS TEACHES OPENLY IN THE TEMPLE

After Jesus' brothers had gone, he went secretly to the festival. The Jewish leaders tried to find him at the festival and kept asking if anyone had seen him.

John 7
10-52

What do you think the people in the crowds said about Jesus. Can you work it out?

Some said   but others said

_ _   _ _   _ _ _   _ _'   _ _   _ _ _

_ _ _ _ _   _ _ _'   _   _ _ _ _ _ _ _ _'

But, Harry, no-one would say anything about him publicly because they were afraid of getting into trouble with the Jewish leaders.

Look, Jess, halfway through the festival, Jesus went up to the temple and began to teach.

That gave the Jewish leaders a real surprise. You see, Harry, he knew a lot. They just couldn't understand how he knew so much when he hadn't studied everything they'd studied.

Jesus told them that his teaching wasn't his own. It came from God. He accused them of trying to kill him. What did some of the people in Jerusalem say? Work out the puzzle by going round the circle. Start at the arrow and fill in the gaps. All the words are separated by other letters - take these letters and put them into the last word. The first letter of the first word and the first letter of the last word are done for you.

Isn'tmthisethesmanstheyiareatrynghtomkill?eHereshesisspeakingapublicly,handmtheyaresnotssayinggaawordhtomhim.eCansitsbeithataourhleadersmknowethatshesreallyiisatheh.

I ___ ____ ____ ____

____ ____ ____ ____

____ . ____ ____ ___

____ ____ ____ ____ —— ,

____ ____ ____ ____

____ . ____ ___ ___ ____

____ ____ ____ ___ ____

___ _____ ___ ___

M_____

But, how could he be who he said he was? After all, they knew where Jesus came from.

They thought that the Messiah would just appear, and that no-one would know where he came from. But in the circle puzzle below you will find out what Jesus said. Write the words out in full beside the circles. Note down the letters that are the odd ones out to find out what the Jewish leaders were planning to do to Jesus.

Answer:_____

Yes you know me, And you know where I come from. But I represent one you don't know and he is True. I know Him because I have come from him and he sent Me to you.

Jesus said some more things which puzzled them.

What did they think he might do? Rearrange the highlighted letters in the spiral to find out.

Answer: _ _ _ v _ _ _   _ _ _   c _ _ _ _ _y.

Jesus also said this. (To find out what Jesus meant by "living water", read the highlighted letters in the spiral to find out.)

I will be here for A little longer and THen I will go back to the one who sent me. You will look for me but you won't find me. And you won't be able to come where I am.

Answer: _ _ _ _   _p _ _ _ _

For the scriptures say that streams of living water will flow out from within. If you are thirsty, come to me! If you believe in me, come and drink!

The crowds couldn't decide who Jesus was. Some thought he was the Messiah and others didn't. The temple guards went to arrest Jesus, but didn't. "We've never heard anyone talk like this," they said.

JESUS HEALS A MAN BORN BLIND

Jess and I are reading another story about Jesus. He was walking along one day, when he saw a man who had been born blind. The disciples seemed to think that he was blind because he or his parents had sinned.

Yes Harry, but Jesus soon put them right. He said that the man had been born blind so that the power of God could be seen in him. To work out what happened take the initial letters of the objects and insert these into the gaps.

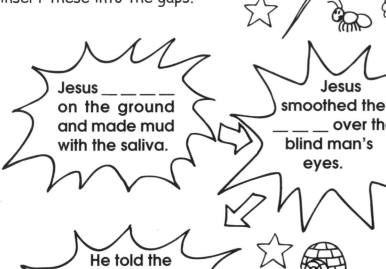

Jesus _ _ _ _ on the ground and made mud with the saliva.

Jesus smoothed the _ _ _ over the blind man's eyes.

He told the man to go and wash at the pool of _ _ _ _ _ _ _

Can you help the blind man find the way to the Pool?

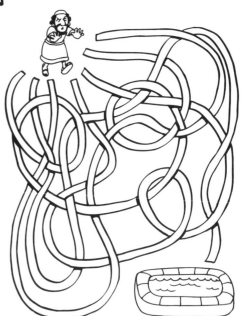

The man went and washed at the pool, and he was healed. Everyone who knew asked, "Is this the same man?" He insisted that he was - and told them what had happened. So they took him to the Pharisees and told them. What happened next?

Some said:

This man Jesus is not from God because he's working on the Sabbath.

28

But how could an ordinary sinner do these miraculous signs.

The man who'd been blind said...

I think he's a prophet.

His parents said...

We know he is our son and that he was born blind. But we don't know how he can see or who healed him. Why don't you ask him?

The man exclaimed...

I don't know whether Jesus is a sinner. One thing I do know. I was blind but now I see.

The Pharisees were angry and they cursed the man. They said:

We are disciples of Moses. We knew God spoke to Moses, but as for this man, we don't know anything about him.

The Pharisees were furious and threw the man out of the temple. But he believed in Jesus and worshipped him.

That's remarkable. He healed my eyes, but you don't know anything about him. Well, God doesn't listen to sinners but he hears those who worship and obey him. No-one has ever heard of a blind man being healed. If this man were not from God he couldn't do it.

THE GOOD SHEPHERD

John 10: 1-16

Hi there! Jess and I are discovering that Jesus often used picture language to describe who he was.

That's right! And in John's gospel we've found out that he sometimes called himself the Shepherd and the sheep were his followers. Click has emailed us some Bible facts below. Can you match the Bible fact to the correct part of the picture below?

1. The man who sneaks over the wall of the sheepfold instead of going through the gate is a thief and a robber.

2. The Shepherd enters through the gate and the gatekeeper opens the gate for him.

3. The sheep hear the shepherd's voice and come to him. He calls his own sheep by name and they come to him.

So - as you will see from the picture there were no sheep dogs... but there were wild wolves to watch out for! The Shepherd would just call his sheep and the sheep, who knew his voice, would simply follow him! Amazing! Click's emailed me another Bible fact ... look at this...

When he has gathered his own flock, the shepherd walks ahead of them. The sheep follow the shepherd because they know his voice. But they will run from a stranger because they don't recognise his voice.

Jesus said, "I am the good shepherd.

The good shepherd lays down his life for the sheep. When a hired helper sees a wolf coming, he runs away because he doesn't care for the sheep. The wolf then attacks and scatters the flock.

He said, "I know my own sheep and they know me, just as my Father knows me and I know my Father. And I lay down my life for the sheep.

I have other sheep that are not in this sheepfold and I must bring them too. They will listen to my voice and there will be one flock and one shepherd.

But what does all this mean Jess?

Well Harry - it's like this- a good shepherd might die to protect his sheep from a wolf. But Jesus is even better! He is called *The Good Shepherd* as he willingly gave his life to save us from our sin. When we love and follow him we belong to him, we are part of his flock. There are other people who haven't yet heard about Jesus Christ. Jesus will

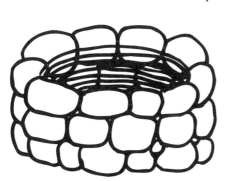

bring them into his flock too. We can all be part of God's plan to bring the good news of Jesus Christ to the whole world. Perhaps God will tell you to become a preacher or a missionary ... or perhaps he will use you to be a missionary to your own family and friends. He can use you anytime, anywhere, we just have to give our lives to God and in Jesus' name ask him to forgive us for our sins.

THE DEATH OF LAZARUS

John 11 — HOLY BIBLE

Look at this Harry - We've got another story from Click. He's found this one in John Chapter 11. Let's investigate! At the bottom of the scroll is a code to work out - it spells out a name Jesus gave himself.

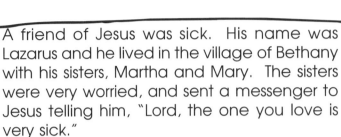

A friend of Jesus was sick. His name was Lazarus and he lived in the village of Bethany with his sisters, Martha and Mary. The sisters were very worried, and sent a messenger to Jesus telling him, "Lord, the one you love is very sick."

When Jesus heard the message, he said, "Lazarus's sickness will not end in death. No, it is for God's glory. I, the Son of God will receive glory from this."

Even though Jesus loved Lazarus and his sisters, he stayed where he was for two days. Then he said to the disciples, "Let's go back to Judea."

The disciples were amazed. "But Teacher," they said, "only a few days ago the Jewish leaders tried to stone you, and now you are going back there?"

Jesus then told the disciples that Lazarus had fallen asleep and that he was going to wake him up.

The disciples said to Jesus, "If he is sleeping then he will get better. They didn't realise that Jesus meant Lazarus had died, so he told them plainly, "Lazarus is dead... Come on, Let's go and see him."

Thomas said to the other disciples, "Let's go too - and die with Jesus."

What did the code spell out?

_ _ _ _ _ _ _ _ _ _

_ _ _ _ _ _ _ _ _

At the grave of Lazarus Jesus shouts a command - to work it out use the code and then fill in the gaps.

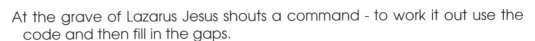

_ _ _ _ _ _ _ _ _ _ _ _

 When Jesus arrived at Bethany Lazarus had been dead for four days. Many people had arrived to comfort Martha and Mary. When Martha heard that Jesus was coming she went to see him. "Lord, if you had been here, Lazarus would not have died. But even now, I know that God will give you whatever you ask." Jesus said, "Your brother will rise again,"

but Martha thought that Jesus meant that he would rise on the resurrection day. Jesus said, "I am the resurrection and the life. Whoever believes in me, even though he dies, will live again. Do you believe this, Martha?"

"Yes Lord," she said. "I have always believed that you are the Christ, the Son of God, who has come into the world." Then Martha went to Mary. "Mary," she said, "The Teacher is here and wants to see you."

Mary left quickly, but when the people saw her go, they thought that she was going to Lazarus's grave to weep. So they followed her. When Mary saw Jesus, she said, "Lord, if you had been here, my brother would not have died."

When Jesus saw Mary and the others weeping, he was deeply moved and troubled. "Where have you put him?" he asked.

"Come and see," they said. Then Jesus wept. The people who were near to him said, "See how much he loved him." But some said, "He opened the eyes of a blind man. Couldn't he have kept this man from dying?"

They came to the grave which was a cave with a stone rolled across the entrance, and Jesus said, "Roll the stone aside."

Martha was surprised. "Lord," she said, "the smell will be terrible by now." But Jesus replied, "Didn't I tell you that if you believe, you will see God's glory?" So they rolled aside the stone.

Jesus said, "Father, thank you for hearing me. I know that you always hear me but I said it for the sake of all these people so that they will believe you sent me."

Then Jesus shouted, "Lazarus, come out!" Lazarus came out, bound in grave clothes, his face wrapped in a head cloth. And Jesus said to them,

To find out what Jesus said turn this sentence back to front - if you have a mirror near by and can use it that might help you work it out!

Unwrap him and let him go

Well, we've done the story - now it's time to investigate the passage a little further. Click has a crossword for us! Take your time and only use the answers at the back of the book if you're really stuck.

Across

1. A sister of Lazarus.
4. Lazarus was buried in one of these.
6. Lazarus was this before he died.
7. It was rolled away from Lazarus' tomb.
11. "The teacher wants to see _ _ _."
12. John the Baptist wanted to make Jesus this.
14. Lazarus was healed so that God would receive it.
15. Land beside the sea.
17. Not "he".
18. Jesus felt this for Lazarus.
19. Lazarus was this in relation to Martha and Mary.
22. A word meaning to look at or notice something.
24. Not asleep.
25. Not ever.

Down

1. The sisters sent one to Jesus.
3. A relative of the horse but with longer ears.
4. Jesus stayed where he was for this number of days.
5. The number of days Lazarus had been dead before Jesus came.
8. A name given to Jesus in the story.
9. They were opened on the Sabbath in the previous story.
10. Lazarus' death caused Martha and Mary to do this.
12. They thought Mary was going to it.
13. A part of the foot.
16. You might play this with a musical instrument.
18. An untruth.
20. It has a trunk and branches.
21. Jesus said that Lazarus would do this again.
22. Jesus was this in relation to God.
23. A body part used for hearing.

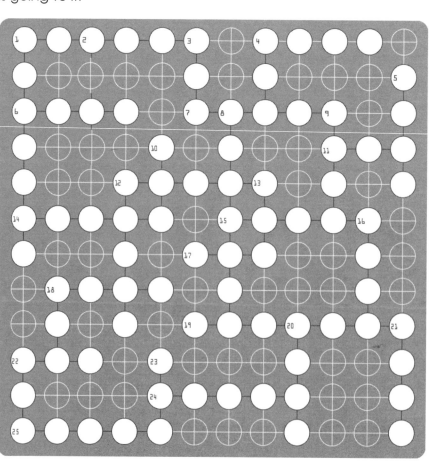

34

After Lazarus was raised from the dead, lots of people who had been there believed in Jesus.

But some told the Pharisees. They called a meeting together with the leading priests to discuss what to do. Use the clock puzzle to find out what they said.

10pm 7am 12am 7pm   12am 5pm 4am   10pm 4am

12am 2am 2am 2pm 12pm 3pm 11am 8am 6pm 7am 8am 1pm 6am?

7am 4am 5pm 4am   8am 6pm   7pm 7am 8am 6pm   12pm 12am 1pm

3pm 4am 5pm 5am 2pm 5pm 12pm 8am 1pm 6am   12pm 12am 1pm 11pm

12pm 8am 5pm 12am 2am 8pm 11am 2pm 8pm 6pm   6pm 8am 6am 1pm 6pm

8am 5am   10pm 4am   11am 4am 7pm   7am 8am 12pm   6am 2pm   2pm 1pm

11am 8am 10am 4am   7pm 7am 8am 6pm   4am 9pm 4am 5pm 11pm 2pm 1pm 4am

10pm 8am 11am 11am   1am 4am 11am 8am 4am 9pm 4am   8am 1pm   7am 8am 12pm

____ ___ __ _____ ____? __

____ ___ _____ ____ _____ _

_____. __ __ ___ ___ __ __ ____ ____,

_____ ____ _____ __ ___.

They were very worried! You see, they thought that if this happened, the Roman army of occupation would come and destroy their temple and their nation.

Caiaphas the high priest had other ideas, though ... work out the code to discover what it was that Caiaphas said...

11pm 2pm 8pm   10am 1pm 2pm 10pm   1pm 2pm 7pm 7am 8am 1pm 6am

12am 7pm   12am 11am 11am!   11pm 2pm 8pm   3am 2pm   1pm 2pm 7pm

5pm 4am 12am 11am 8am 6pm 4am   7pm 7am 12am 7pm   8am 7pm   8am 6pm

1am 4am 7pm 7pm 4am 5pm   5am 2pm 5pm   11pm 2pm 8pm   7pm 7am 12am 7pm

2pm 1pm 4am   12pm 12am 1pm   3am 8am 4am 6pm   5am 2pm 5pm   7pm 7am 4am

3pm 4am 2pm 3pm 11am 4am   7pm 7am 12am 1pm   7pm 7am 12am 7pm   7pm 7am 4am

10pm 7am 2pm 11am 4am   1pm 12am 7pm 8am 2pm 1pm

3pm 4am 5pm 8am 6pm 7am 4am 6pm

___ ____ _____ __ ___! ___ __ ___

_____ ____ __ __ _____ ___ ___ ____

___ ___ ___ ___ ___ _____ ____ ____

___ _____ _____ _____.

It was no accident that Caiaphas said these words. He had been inspired by God to say them. It was a prediction that Jesus' death would not just be for Israel, but to draw together all God's children around the world.

So, because they were plotting his death, Jesus stopped his public ministry. He went with his disciples to the village of Ephraim, near the wilderness.

JESUS ANOINTED AT BETHANY

It's now chapter 12 and six days before the Passover begins. Jesus is now at Bethany where Lazarus lived. What happens next? To find out the name of the disciple who is a thief use the code at the bottom of the story.

John 12: 1-10

A dinner was made in Jesus' honour, and Martha served, while Lazarus sat at the table with Jesus. Then Mary took a twelve ounce jar of expensive perfume made from essence of nard. She anointed Jesus' feet with it and wiped them with her hair. Soon the house was filled with the fragrance.

One of the disciples said, "That perfume was worth a year's wages. Why wasn't it sold and given to the poor?" He didn't say this because he cared about the poor. He was a thief who was in charge of the disciples' funds, and he used to help himself to the money.

Jesus said, "Leave her alone. She did this in preparation for my burial. You will always have the poor among you, but you won't always have me."

A large crowd of Jews heard that Jesus was there, and they flocked to see him and also Lazarus. Then the leading priests decided to kill Lazarus too, for it was because of him that many Jews were putting their faith in Jesus.

___ ___ ___ ___ ___ ___   ___ ___ ___ ___ ___ ___ ___ ___

Have a look at this Alphabet tree. There is a question for every letter of the alphabet. If you think you have the right answer write it into the correct leaf on the tree. You can always check your answers at the back of the book when you're finished.

A. Mary did this to Jesus' feet.
B. Lazarus' home village.
C. They were carried out at Passover.
D. It was given in Jesus' honour.
E. The perfume was this.
F. Mary wiped them.
G. Jesus' Father.
H. Mary wiped away perfume with it.
I. A thief.
J. A perfume container.
K. The priests plotted to do this to Jesus.
L. "L_ _ _ _ her alone!"
M. Judas was in charge of it.
N. The perfume was made from this essence.

O. Weights mentioned in the story.
P. The name for the special feast.
Q. Not slow.
R. R _ _ _ _ _ from the dead.
S. Judas said they should do this with the perfume.
T. Lazarus sat here to eat with Jesus.
U. The opposite of over.
V. Another word for expensive.
W. Mary did this with her hair.
X. _ _ x The number of days before the festival.
Y. A measurement of time used to describe the value of the perfume.
Z. One of Jesus's table companions has this letter in his name. Who is he?

THE TRIUMPHAL ENTRY

John 12: 12-19

The day after, word got out that Jesus was on his way to Jerusalem. So a huge crowd of Passover visitors went to meet him. They waved palm branches and shouted ... Well, can you work it out? Follow the arrows and put the signs into the right order.

King of Israel

Bless the one →

Who comes in

Hail to the ←

Praise God

the name of →

the Lord ↑

Answer: _____

_____

Then Jesus rode into Jerusalem on a young donkey and this fulfilled a prophecy.

people →

of Israel ↓

your King

donkey's ↓

Don't →

be afraid ↑

Look →

is coming →

sitting on a ↑

colt

Answer: _____

_____

But what the disciples didn't realise was that this event had been foretold long before Jesus was born. It was only much later after Jesus had died that they realised. And do you know what the Pharisees said to each other when they saw it all?

We've lost. Look! The whole world has gone after him.

THE JEWS CONTINUE IN THEIR UNBELIEF

This is an amazing investigation isn't it Jess?

Yes but what I think is amazing is that even when Jesus had done miraculous signs, some people would still not believe him. The prophet Isaiah said long before Jesus came that peoples' eyes would be blinded to the truth and their hearts would not understand.

But Jess, some people did believe. Even some leaders. But because they were afraid that the Pharisees would throw them out of the synagogue, they kept quiet about it. Jesus said , "When a man believes in me, he also believes in the one who sent me." Match up the words to discover what else he said.

John 12:37-46

HOLY BIBLE

_____

_____

_____

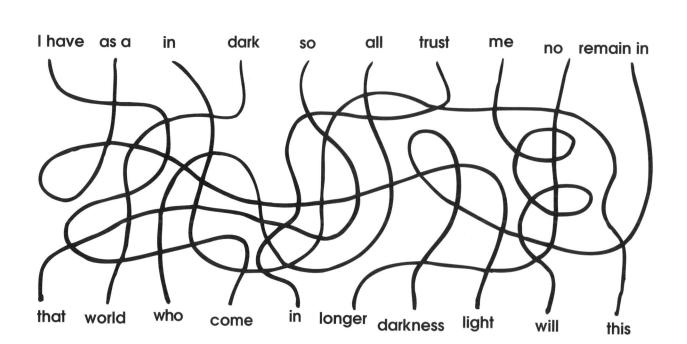

I have   as a   in   dark   so   all   trust   me   no   remain in

that   world   who   come   in   longer   darkness   light   will   this

JESUS WASHES HIS DISCIPLES FEET

John 13: 1-17

Harry and I are now onto chapter 13. It was almost time for the Passover celebration, and Jesus knew that it would soon be time to leave the world and go back to his Father.

But look at this Jess! It was time for supper, and the Devil had already got Judas Iscariot to betray Jesus. Let's see what happened next.

Jesus got up from the table, took off his robe, wrapped a towel around his waist and poured water into a basin. Then he began to wash the disciples' feet and to wipe them with a towel. This was a job always done

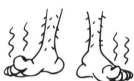

by the lowest of the servants, and Peter just couldn't understand it. "You will never wash my feet!" But Jesus said, "You won't belong to me unless I wash you." And you know what Peter said?

Jesus said, "A person who has washed all over does not need to wash except for the feet. And you are clean, but not all of you." Jesus knew that Judas was going to betray him. Then Jesus put on his robe again and asked the disciples

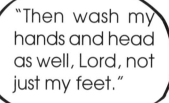

"Then wash my hands and head as well, Lord, not just my feet."

if they understood what he'd done for them. He wanted them to know that a servant isn't greater than his master , or messenger more important than the one who sends him. Can you work out what he said? Work out what letters are missing by looking at the pictures below. Then replace these letters into the sentence. There is a number beside each picture to tell you how many times each letter goes in.

(11) (18) (8) (15) (9)

_ h_v_ s_t y_ _ _n _x_mpl_ th_t y_ _

sh_ _ld d_ _s _ h_v_ d_n_ f_r y_ _. _ t_ll

y_ _ th_ tr_th, n_ s_rv_nt _s gr_ _t_r th_n h_s

m_st_r. N_w th_t y_ _ kn_w th_s_ th_ngs, y_ _

w_ll b_ bl_ss_d _f y_ _ d_ th_m. (Verses 15-17)

41

JESUS PREDICTS HIS BETRAYAL

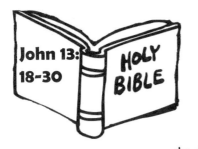

John 13: 18-30 — HOLY BIBLE

A long time before Jesus was born, his betrayal was mentioned in the book of Psalms. And Jesus told his disciples about it. Write down the first letter, miss two, then write the next letter down and continue to the end to find out what was said.

Answer:

_ _ _   _ _ _

_ _ _

_ _ _ _ _ _

_ _   _ _ _ _

_ _ _

_ _ _ _ _ _

_ _ _ _ _ _ _

_ _.

```
T O L H E G E F M O J C
N G U E S L W B I H D A
O K C S U T H C N A M I
R T V E Q U S G J M W K
Y O T F W E O L E O M U
D B I H Z N A P A S Y O
T A J U X T R F R N D U
E C H D A L A G N G R T
A Z P I M B N V O S E C
T N A M O R E
```

Jesus was really troubled, and said to his disciples, "I tell you the truth, one of you is going to betray me." As you can guess, the disciples were wondering who on earth would do it. "It is the one to whom I give this bread when I have dipped it in the sauce," Jesus said. As Judas took the bread, Satan entered him. Find out what Jesus said by taking the first letter, miss two letters and write the next one down and continue to the end.

```
T  O  L  H  E  G  E  F  M  O  J  C
N  G  U  E  S  L  W  B  I  H  D  A
O  K  C  V  U  T  H  C  N  A  M  I
R  T  V  E  Q  U  S  G  J  M  W  K
Y  O  T  F  W  N  O  L  E  O  M  U
D  B  I  H  N  N  A  P  A  S  Y  O
T  A  J  U  X  T  P  R  R  N  D  U
E  C  H  D  A  L  F  N  N  G  R  T
A  Z  P  I  M  B  G  G  O  S  E  T
N  A  M  O  R  E  V     S
```

Answer: _ _ _ _ _ _,   _ _   _ _   _ _   _ _ _

JESUS PREDICTS PETER'S DENIAL

Judas left and Jesus told the disciples that he, the Son of man, was about to be glorified. He would not be with them much longer. He gave a new commandment. Follow the bees to find out what it was.

Love each you, have loved you should Just as I love other. other. each

Now, follow the butterflies to find out what else he said to them.

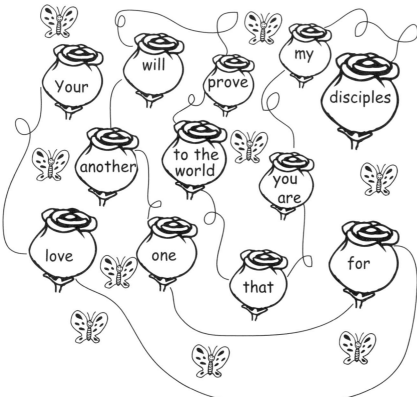

Your will prove my disciples another to the world you are love one that for

Peter wanted to know where Jesus was going, so Jesus said,

"You can't go with me now, but you will follow me later."
"But Lord, Why can't I follow you now? I am ready to die for you," Peter said. And do you know what Jesus said next? "Before the cock crows, you will disown me three times."

JESUS, THE WAY TO THE FATHER

Jesus said many things to encourage his disciples before he died. Click has found some...

John 14: 1-31

There are many rooms in my Father's home, and I am going to prepare a place for you ... When everything is ready, I will come and get you so that you will always be with me.

I am the way, the truth and the life. No-one can come to the Father except through me.

Anyone who believes in me will do the same works I have done and even greater works ... You may ask for anything in my name and I will do it.

If you love me, obey my commandments. I will ask the Father and he will give you another Counsellor, the Holy Spirit, who will never leave you ... He will teach you everything.

Those who love me will obey my teaching. My Father will love them and will come to them and live with them.

Jesus told the disciples that he would leave them a gift. Answer the questions and the vertical column will reveal what it was.

1. Jesus went ahead to prepare one.
2. The Holy Spirit will never do this.
3. I am the _ _ _.
4. Another name for the Holy Spirit.
5. People only come to the Father through him.
6. People who love Jesus will do this.
7. Jesus is the truth and the _ _ _ _.
8. If you love Jesus you will keep them.
9. Jesus said that the person who does this will do greater works than him.
10. People who love Jesus will obey it.
11. Jesus' followers.

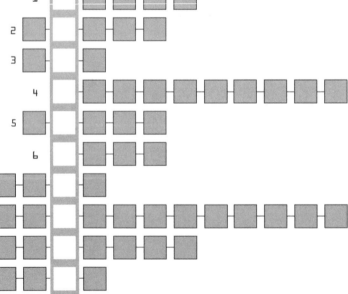

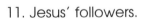

44

JESUS THE TRUE VINE

Harry and I are looking at chapter 15 now. Jesus used the picture of fruit to describe what his followers produce when they live their lives for him.
In the pictures below can you find a duck, an ant, a butterfly and a caterpillar?

Jesus said, "I am the true vine and my Father is the gardener. He cuts off every branch that doesn't produce fruit. He prunes those that do bear fruit so that they will produce more.

I am the vine and you are the branches. If you remain in me, you will bear much fruit. But apart from me you can do nothing. If anyone doesn't remain in me he is like a useless branch and withers. These branches are gathered into a pile and are burned.

Jesus said, "I chose you and I appointed you to go and produce fruit that will last. Then my Father will give you whatever you ask for in my name."

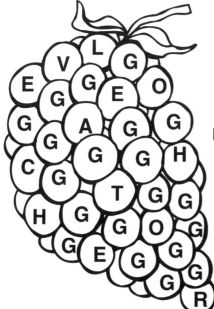

Look at the grapes on the vine. Take out all the letter G's and arrange the letters you have left into a command given by Jesus.

Answer: _ _ _ _   _ _ _ _

_ _ _ _ _

THE WORK OF THE HOLY SPIRIT -

Click has downloaded some information from chapter 16 for us ... but it's a little bit different. Follow the route and you can find out what Click has discovered.

John 16: 1-16

Start here

Jesus said to the disciples, "Now I am going back to him who sent me. If I don't go

Dead End

the Counsellor, the Holy Spirit, won't come to you. If I do go away He will

Dead End

He will convince the world of sin and of God's righteousness and of the coming judgement. The world's sin is

come because I will send him to you. And when he comes

Dead End

He will bring glory to me by showing you whatever he receives from me.

Dead End

not believing in me ... When the Spirit of truth comes

Dead End

speak on his own. He will tell you what he has heard and he will tell you about the future

Dead End

He will guide you in all truth. He will not

Dead End

JESUS PRAYS FOR HIS DISCIPLES

Before Jesus died, he prayed for his disciples and for all who would come to believe in him. He asked God to take care of them, to make them pure and holy, and to protect them from Satan. He also prayed that they would be brought to complete unity. Can you find out the reason why?

_ _   _ _ _   _ _ _ _   _ _ _ _ _   _ _ _ _   _ _

_ _   _ _ _   _ _ _ _   _ _ _   _ _ _ _ _   _ _

_ _ _   _ _   _ _ _ _   _ _ _   _ _ _ _ _   _ _

JESUS IS BETRAYED AND ARRESTED

After praying, Jesus and his disciples crossed the Kidron valley and went into an olive grove. Judas Iscariot knew where they were going. The priests and Pharisees had given Judas some guards and soldiers. They came into the olive grove carrying torches, lanterns and weapons.

Jesus knew what was going to happen and he went to meet them. "Who are you looking for?" he asked. They said, "Jesus of Nazareth." "I am he," said Jesus. And you know what happened next? They all fell to the ground! Jesus spoke again - he said, "As I'm the one you want, let these others go." Then Simon-Peter, who had a sword, cut off the right ear of Malchus, the High Priest's servant. Jesus said, "Put your sword away. Shall I not drink the cup the Father has given me?"

Jesus knew that it was the time for him to be captured. He wasn't going to run away, and he didn't want any violence. Can you find the following words in the wordsearch?

lantern, sword, torch, Malchus, ear, Judas, Jesus, Kidron, soldiers, Pharisees.

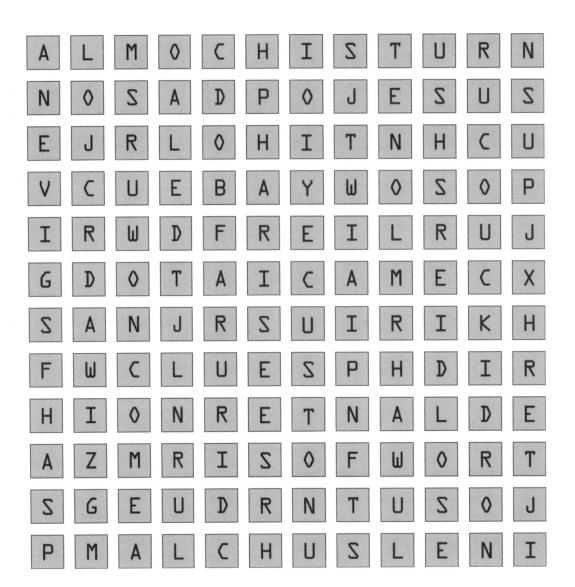

A	L	M	O	C	H	I	S	T	U	R	N
N	O	S	A	D	P	O	J	E	S	U	S
E	J	R	L	O	H	I	T	N	H	C	U
V	C	U	E	B	A	Y	W	O	S	O	P
I	R	W	D	F	R	E	I	L	R	U	J
G	D	O	T	A	I	C	A	M	E	C	X
S	A	N	J	R	S	U	I	R	I	K	H
F	W	C	L	U	E	S	P	H	D	I	R
H	I	O	N	R	E	T	N	A	L	D	E
A	Z	M	R	I	S	O	F	W	O	R	T
S	G	E	U	D	R	N	T	U	S	O	J
P	M	A	L	C	H	U	S	L	E	N	I

Phew! This investigation
is hard work Jess!

Yes! I know –
but come on
Harry we're
almost there –
it's not far to
go now!

JESUS TAKEN TO ANNAS AND PETER'S DENIALS

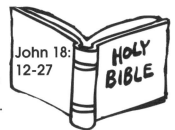

John 18: 12-27

Click has some more information on where Jesus went next. He was taken to Annas, the father-in-law of Caiaphas, the high priest that year.

It was Caiaphas who had said it was better for one person to die for all the people. Read the rest of the story for yourself.

Peter was allowed into the courtyard of the house. A woman saw Peter and recognised him. "Aren't you one of Jesus' disciples?" she asked. "No," said Peter, "I am not." It was cold, and the servants were standing around a fire. Peter stood and warmed himself too. Back indoors, the High Priest questioned Jesus about his teachings. Jesus said, "What I teach is widely known because I have preached often in the Temple and the synagogues. I teach nothing privately that I haven't said in public." Then Jesus said, "Why are you asking these questions? Ask the people who heard me - they know what I said."

At this, one of the temple guards struck Jesus in the face. "Is this the way to answer the High Priest?" he demanded.

Jesus said, "If I said anything wrong, you should give evidence for it. I spoke the truth, so why did you strike me?"

Outside, Peter was asked again, "Aren't you one of the disciples?" "I am not," he said. But one of the servants who was a relative of the man whose ear Peter had cut off, said, "Didn't I see you in the olive grove with Jesus?" Peter denied it again, and at that moment a cock crowed.

Can you find the cockerel and three mice in this picture?

49

JESUS' TRIAL BEFORE PILATE

Click has faxed the next update.

John 18: 28-40 HOLY BIBLE

Yes, Harry - look at this - In the early hours of the morning, Jesus was taken to Pilate, the Roman governor. Pilate told the Jews to judge him by their own laws. "But only the Romans are allowed to execute someone," they said. Pilate said to Jesus, "Are you the King of the Jews?" Jesus said, "Is that your own idea, or did others tell you about me?" "Am I a Jew?" asked Pilate. "Your own people brought you here. What have you done?" Jesus told Pilate that he wasn't an earthly king - his kingdom was not of this world. "You are a king, then?" Pilate asked. "You say I am a king and you are right. I was born for that purpose," said Jesus. *What else did he say? Do the puzzle to find out.*

a	a3	c4	e9	f1	f5	
e	a5	b10	d1	d4	d11	e6	f12
i	a1	a10	e4	f3	f7	
o	a7	b7	b12	c9	c11	e1
u	b3	d7	f11			

① ② ③ ④ ⑤ ⑥ ⑦ ⑧ ⑨ ⑩ ⑪ ⑫

a: c m t b r n g
b: t r t h t t h w
c: r l d l l w h l v
d: t h t r t h r c
e: g n s t h t w h
f: t s y s t r

_____

_____

"What is truth?" Pilate asked. Then he went out to the Jews and told them that he found no basis for a charge against Jesus. "It's your custom for me to release a prisoner at Passover. Do you want me to release the King of the Jews?" he asked. But they shouted back, "No! Not him! Give us Barabbas!"

JESUS IS SENTENCED TO DEATH

John 19:1-16

Jesus had done nothing wrong, but he was treated with real cruelty. Pilate had him flogged with a lead-tipped whip which would have cut his back into ribbons. Then the soldiers made him wear a crown of long, sharp thorns on his head. And they put a royal purple robe on him. They mocked him and hit him on the face.

Hail, King of the Jews!

Then Pilate went outside and said...

I'm going to bring him out to you now, but I want you to understand that I find him not guilty.

Jesus was brought out, and the leading priests and temple guards started shouting.

Crucify! Crucify!

But Pilate said You crucify him! He is not guilty! The Jewish leaders insisted that by their law he should die because he called himself the son of God. And that made Pilate afraid. He took Jesus back into the palace and spoke to him.

Can you work out Jesus' reply? Fill in the missing o's and u's.

Y _ _ w _ _ ld have n _

p _ wer _ ver me unless it

were fr _ m ab _ ve. S _ the

_ ne wh _ br _ _ ght me t _

y _ _ is g _ ilty _ f a greater sin.

Where do you come from? Why won't you talk to me? Don't you realise that I have the power to free you or crucify you?

Then Pilate tried to let Jesus go free, but the Jewish leaders said ...

If you let him go, you are no friend of Caesar. Anyone who says he is a king is a rebel against Caesar.

Then Pilate brought Jesus out again. He sat down on the Judges seat at a place called the Stone Pavement. It was about noon on the day of preparation for the Passover.

Here is your king.

But all they said was, "Take him away! Take him away! Crucify him!"

"What? Crucify your king?" Said Pilate. "We have no king but Caesar!" They exclaimed. Then Pilate handed Jesus over to them to be crucified.

CROSSWORD

Across
1. Used to flog Jesus.
6. Not down.
8. Old Testament prophet.
10. _ _ _ _ King of the Jews!
11. Not far.
13. Used to make Jesus' crown.
14. Where Jesus was hit.
15. A measure.
17. Jesus did not do this.
18. Pilate felt this after listening to the Jewish leaders.
19. When did Pilate sit down at the judges seat?
20. The whip was tipped with this.
21. Jesus' mother.

Down:
2. A crown was placed on it.
3. He sat on the Judge's seat.
4. According to this, Jesus must die.
5. Jesus is the Son of _ _ _. John 13:31
7. The colour of the robe.
9. Female chickens.
12. Pilate said he had the power to do this to Jesus.
14. You are no _ _ _ _ _ _ of Caesar.
15. Not out.
16. Pilate said Jesus was not this.
17. What pavement?

THE CRUCIFIXION

The soldiers took Jesus and led him away. Carrying his own cross, Jesus went to the place of the skull. They crucified him there with two others - one on either side of him. Pilate placed a sign over Jesus. It read...

John 19: 17-27

Jesus of Nazareth. King of the Jews

Can you work out which languages they were written in?

_ _ _ _ _ _

_ _ _ _ _

_ _ _ _ _

The chief priests didn't like this. They said, "Don't write "The King of the Jews," but that this man claimed to be king of the Jews." But Pilate said, "What I have written I have written." When the soldiers crucified Jesus, they divided his clothes among the four of them. His robe was seamless and woven in one piece from top to bottom so they threw a dice and gambled to see who would get it.

This fulfilled a scripture which said - (insert )to get the answer

Th _ y d _ v _ d _ d my cl _ th _ s _ m _ ng th _ m _ nd thr _ w

d _ c _ f _ r my r _ b _. (Psalm 22:18)

Near the cross were Jesus' mother, his mother's sister, Mary, the wife of Clopas and Mary Magdalene. When Jesus saw his mother there, beside the disciple he loved, he said, "Dear woman, here is your son," and to the disciple, "Here is your mother." And from that time on, the disciple took her into his home.

THE DEATH OF JESUS

Jesus knew that everything was finished, and to fulfill scripture said, "I am thirsty." So they soaked a sponge in vinegar and put it on a hyssop branch. They lifted it to Jesus' lips, and when he had tasted it, he said, "It is finished."

Then he bowed his head and gave up his spirit. Because the next day was the Sabbath and Passover time the Jewish leaders asked Pilate to have the legs broken and the bodies taken down. So the soldiers broke the legs of the two men crucified with Jesus. But when they came to Jesus he was already dead, so they didn't break his legs. A soldier pierced his side with a spear, and blood and water flowed out. These fulfilled a scripture. Follow the lines to find out what it was.

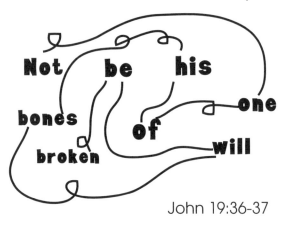

John 19:36-37

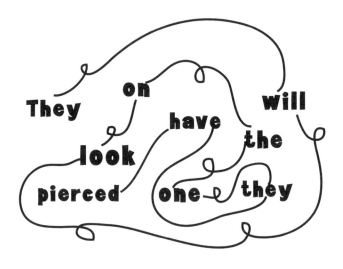

THE BURIAL OF JESUS

Then - Joseph of Arimathea, a secret disciple of Jesus stepped in. He was a secret believer because he was afraid of the Jewish leaders. Anyway, he went to Pilate and asked for permission to take Jesus' body down. Then, when Pilate agreed, he took the body away.

Joseph and Nicodemus took Jesus' body and wrapped it with spices, in strips of linen. Not far from the place where Jesus was crucified, there was a garden with a new tomb. It had never been used before. Because it was the day of preparation before the Passover, they decided to lay Jesus in the tomb.

THE RESURRECTION

On the Sunday morning, while it was still dark, Mary Magdalene went to Jesus' tomb. But the stone had been rolled away! Quickly she ran and found Simon Peter and the disciple Jesus loved.

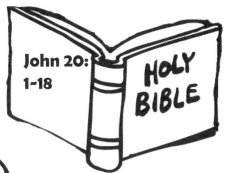

John 20: 1-18

They have taken the Lord's body out of the tomb and I don't know where they've put him.

Peter and the disciple ran to the tomb. The other disciple got there first, and looked into the tomb.

The strips of linen lay there, but he didn't go in. Peter arrived and went straight in. He saw the linen and the cloth which had covered Jesus' head, neatly folded and lying to one side. Then the other disciple went in, and he saw and believed. You see, until then, they hadn't understood the scripture that Jesus would rise from the dead. Peter and the other disciple then went home. Can you spot the four differences between these pictures?

JESUS APPEARS TO MARY MAGDALENE

Mary stood outside the tomb, crying. She looked inside and saw two angels dressed in white. "Why are you crying?" asked one. "Because they've taken away my Lord and I don't know where they've put him," she said. At that moment, she turned round and saw Jesus, but she didn't recognise him. "Why are you crying?" He asked her. "Who are you looking for?" Mary didn't realise who he was and thought he was someone else. She said, "Sir, if you've taken him away, tell me where you've put him and I will get him." "Mary," Jesus said. And she turned towards him and exclaimed, "Teacher!" Jesus said, "Don't cling to me, for I haven't yet returned to the Father. Go instead to my brothers and tell them that I am returning to my Father and your Father, my God and your God." So Mary found the disciples and told them, "I have seen the Lord!" And she gave him his message. Who did Mary think that Jesus was? Answer the questions on the next page and the vertical column will reveal the answer.

1. Mary _ _ _ _ _ _ _ _ _.
2. Mary called Jesus this.
3. Mary was doing this as she stood outside the tomb.
4. What day of the week was it?
5. Who went into the tomb first?
6. What was lying where Jesus' body had been?
7. The angels were dressed in this.
8. Jesus sent Mary to find them.

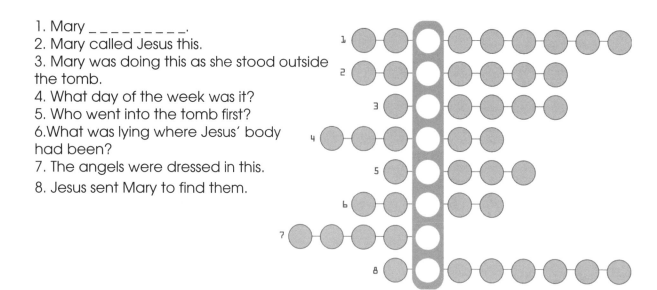

JESUS APPEARS TO HIS DISCIPLES

John 20: 19-29

So Harry we can guess how the disciples felt after Jesus died - probably shocked, heartbroken and afraid of the Jewish leaders. So it's no surprise to find out that on the Sunday evening they were meeting together behind locked doors.

Yes Jess, they were probably all wondering what was going to happen next. Then, suddenly, Jesus was standing there with them! How did he get through the locked door? Jesus said, "Peace be with you!" And then he showed them his hands and his side. Well, they were filled with great joy. Then Jesus spoke. Piece together the jigsaws to find out what he said to them. You can write the answers down on the next page.

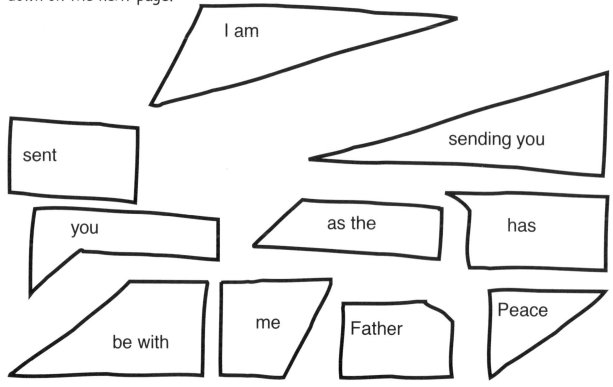

I am

sent

sending you

you

as the

has

be with

me

Father

Peace

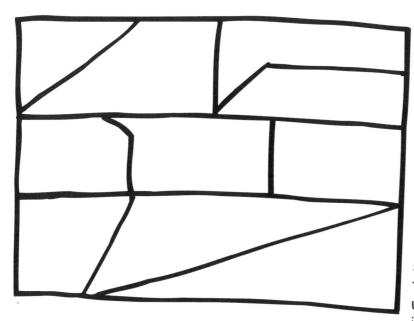

One disciple, Thomas, wasn't there when Jesus came. And when the others told him that they'd seen Jesus, he didn't believe them. "I won't believe it unless I see the nail wounds in his hands and put my fingers into them, and put my hand into the wound in his side." Then, eight days later when the disciples were together again, this time with Thomas, Jesus appeared once more. "Peace be with you," he said. Then he said something to Thomas. Can you work it out? Take the first letter, then miss one and then take the next. Write down your answer in the space provided.

Paubtcydoeufrgfhiinjgkeltrmhneorpegarnsdtsuevewmxyyhzaanbdcsd. Peuftgyhoiujrkhlamnndoipngqtrhsetfwuovuwnxdyjiznambycsdiedfeg.

_____

_____

_____

_____

_____

_____

_____

_____

_____

Then Jesus said,

Well Click says we've to turn the page to find out what it was that Jesus said. He also says that there's a puzzle to do - so let's go!

Work out what Jesus said by inserting the correct vowels in the sentence.

a   e   i   o   u

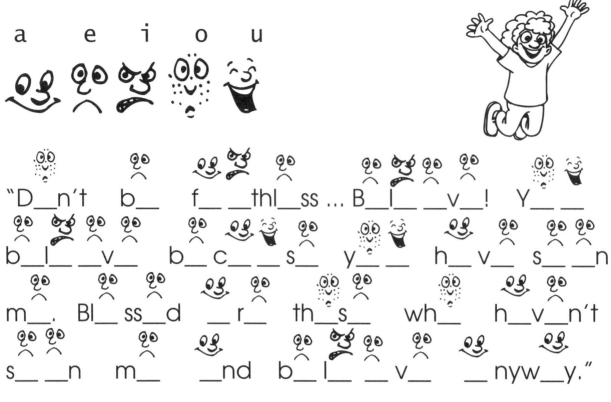

"D_n't b_ f_ _thl_ss ...B_l_ _v_! Y_ _ _

b_l_ _v_ b_c_ _s_ y_ _ h_v_ s_ _n

m_. Bl_ ss_d _r_ th_s_ wh_ h_v_n't

s_ _n m_ _nd b_l_ _v_ _nyw_y."

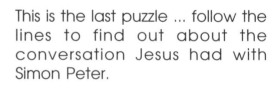

Then one day after breakfast Jesus spoke to Simon Peter.

This is the last puzzle ... follow the lines to find out about the conversation Jesus had with Simon Peter.

Simon Peter replied,

Simon, Son of John, do you love me more than these?"

Yes, Lord, you know I love you.

Then feed my lambs...

Simon Peter again replied,

Simon, Son of John, do you love me?

Simon Peter replied,

Yes, Lord. You know I love you.

Then take care of my sheep...

Simon, Son of John, do you love me?

Lord, you know everything. You know I love you.

Jesus said to Peter, "Feed my sheep. When you were younger you could do as you liked and go wherever you wanted. But when you are older, you will stretch out your hands and others will direct you and take you where you don't want to go. Jesus said this to let Peter know what kind of death he would have to glorify God. Then Jesus said, "Follow me."

When Jesus spoke to Peter about feeding his lambs and caring for his sheep ... what was he talking about? Well he was talking about all those who love and follow him. Do you love the Lord Jesus? Have you thanked him for saving you from your sins when he died on the cross for you? Have you asked God to forgive your sins in the name of the Lord Jesus Christ? If you have then you are one of Jesus' flock. Peter was being told to look after those who trusted in Jesus - to teach them, to tell them about Jesus. This is a very important job. Perhaps you will teach others about Jesus Christ and God's word one day? We should all pray for the people who teach us about Jesus and thank Jesus for coming to this world to show us the way to heaven and to God.

Certificate of Recognition

We've reached the end of the investigation Detectives! Well done everyone! Here is your certificate of Recognition. You deserve it! We're going to log off with some of John's words about his own gospel. John said,

"This is that disciple who saw all these things and who wrote them down. We know that his testimony is true. I suppose that if all the other things Jesus did were written down, the world would not have room for the books that would be written."

As an official member of the Bible Detectives Squad you have been awarded this certificate to mark an excellent result!

Name:

_____

Investigation:

_____

Commenced on :

_____

Completed on:

_____

Signature:

_____

ANSWERS TO JOHN'S GOSPEL - Page numbers in bold.

THE FIRST DISCIPLES. Page **3.** Andrew, Simon, Peter, Philip Nathanael

JESUS CLEARS THE TEMPLE. Page **5.** Zeal for your house consumes me. vertical puzzle 1. sheep, 2. whip, 3. sign, 4. tables, 5. coins, 6. doves, 7. money-changers. Vertical column: his body

JESUS TEACHES NICODEMUS. Page **7.** For God so loved the world that he gave his only son so that everyone who believes in him will not perish but have eternal life. God did not send his son into the world to condemn it but to save it. Page **8** - Those who do what is right come to the light gladly, so everyone can see that they are doing what God wants. **Across:** (1) sins (5) eternal (7) water (9) untie (10) Moses (12) how (14) men (16) life (18) evil (19) hate (20) earth (21) one. **Down:** (2) see (3) truth (4) save (6) trust (8) taste (11) old (12) heaven (13) world (15) night (17) pole.

JOHN THE BAPTIST EXALTS JESUS - Page **10.** He must become greater and greater and I must become less and less. Page **11** Everything. Vertical puzzle 1. heard, 2. true, 3. tells, 4. wrath 5. words, 6. spirit, 7. limit, 8. eternal, 9. everything. Vertical column = authority.

JESUS AND THE SAMARITAN WOMAN - Page **12** If you only knew the gift God has for you and who I am, you would ask me and I would give you living water. Page **14** Now we believe because we have heard for ourselves. Now we know that this man really is the saviour of the world.

THE HEALING AT THE POOL OF BETHESDA - Page **16** Duck, bowl, crutch.

JESUS CLAIMS TO BE THE SON OF GOD - Page **17** Those who listen to my message and believe in God who sent me have eternal life. They will never be condemned for their sins, but they have already passed from death into life. Page **18** (1) scriptures, scriptures, refuse, eternal, life (2) Father, accept, name.

JESUS FEEDS THE FIVE THOUSAND- Page **19** Where shall we buy bread for these people. Eight months wages would not buy enough bread for each one to have a bite. Page **20.** 1. left, 2. two, 3. eight 4. Galilee, 5. loaves, 6. Peter. Diagonal ans: twelve baskets were left. Surely he is the prophet we have been expecting.

JESUS THE BREAD OF LIFE - Page **22** 1. Bread of life, hungry, thirsty. 2. Father, never. 3. everyone, believes. Keyboard puzzle - Lord, to whom would we go? Only you have the words that give eternal life. We believe them and we know you are the holy one of God.

JESUS AND HIS BROTHERS - Page **23** If you can do such wonderful things, prove it to the world. Page **24** The world can't hate you, but it hates me because I accuse it of sin and evil.

JESUS TEACHES OPENLY IN THE TEMPLE - Page **25** He is a good man. No, he is a deceiver. Page **26** Can it be that our leaders know that he really is the Messiah? Page **27** Arrest him. Leaving the country. Holy Spirit.

JESUS HEALS A MAN BORN BLIND - Page **28** spat, mud, Siloam.

THE DEATH OF LAZARUS - Page **32** Resurrection and the Life. Page **33** Lazarus come out. Page **34** Crossword - **Across:** (1) Martha (4) tomb (6) sick (7) stone (11) you (12) great (14) glory (15) coast (17) she (18) love (19) brother (22) see (24) awake (25) never. **Down:** (1) Message (3) ass (4) two (5) four (8) teacher (9) eyes (10) cry (12) grave (13) toe (16) tune (18) lie (20) tree (21) rise (22) son (23) ear. Page **35** What are we accomplishing here? Here is this man performing many miraculous signs. If we let him go on like this, everyone will believe in him. Page **36** You know nothing at all! You do not realise that it is better for you that one man dies for the people than that the whole nation perishes.

JESUS ANOINTED AT BETHANY - Page **37** Judas Iscariot. Page **38** a. anointed, b. Bethany, c. ceremonies, d. dinner, e. expensive, f. feet, g. God, h. hair, i. Iscariot, j. jar, k. kill, l. leave, m. money, n. nard, o. ounces, p. passover, q. quick r. raised, s. sell, t. table, u. under, v. valuable, w. wiped, x. six, y. year, z. Lazarus.

THE TRIUMPHAL ENTRY - Page **39** Praise God! Bless the one who comes in the name of the Lord. Hail to the king of Israel. Don't be afraid, people of Israel. Look, your king is coming, sitting on a donkey's colt.

THE JEWS CONTINUE IN THEIR UNBELIEF - Page **40** I have come as a light in this dark world so that all who trust in me will no longer remain in darkness.

JESUS WASHES HIS DISCIPLES' FEET - Page **41** I have set you an example that you should do as I have done for you. I tell you the truth, no servant is greater than his master. Now that you know these things, you will be blessed if you do them.

JESUS PREDICTS HIS BETRAYAL - Page **42** The one who shares my food has turned against me. Hurry, do it now.

JESUS PREDICTS PETER'S DENIAL - Page **43** Love each other. Just as I have loved you, you should love each other. Your love for one another will prove to the world that you are my disciples.

JESUS, THE WAY TO THE FATHER - Page **44** 1. place, 2. leave, 3. way, 4. counsellor 5. Jesus, 6. obey, 7. life, 8. commandments 9. believes, 10. teaching, 11. disciples. Vertical column: Peace of Mind

JESUS, THE TRUE VINE - Page **45** Love each other

JESUS PRAYS FOR HIS DISCIPLES - Page **47** To let the world know that you sent me and have loved them even as you have loved me.

JESUS' TRIAL BEFORE PILATE - Page **50** I came to bring truth to the world. All who love the truth recognise that what I say is true.

JESUS SENTENCED TO DEATH - Page **51** You would have no power over me unless it were from above. So the one who brought me to you is guilty of a greater sin. Page **52 Across:** (1) whip (6) up (8) Isaiah (10) hail (11) near (13) thorns (14) face (15) inch (17) sin (18) afraid (19) noon (20) lead (21) Mary **Down:** (2) head (3) Pilate, (4) law (5) man (7) purple (9) hens (12) crucify (14) friend (15) in (16) guilty (17) stone

THE CRUCIFIXION - Page **53** Hebrew, Latin, Greek. They divided my clothes among them and threw dice for my robe

THE DEATH OF JESUS - Page **54** Not one of his bones will be broken. They will look on the one they have pierced.

THE RESURRECTION - Page **55** Ducks, Butterflys, Coat, Hat.

JESUS APPEARS TO MARY MAGDALENE - Page **56** 1. Magdalene, 2. Teacher, 3. crying, 4. Sunday, 5. Peter, 6. linen, 7. white 8. brothers. Vertical column: gardener

JESUS APPEARS TO THE DISCIPLES - Page **57** Peace be with you. As the Father has sent me I am sending you. Put your finger here and see my hands. Put your hand in the wound in my side. 58. Don't be faithless ... believe! You believe because you have seen me. Blessed are those who haven't seen me and believe anyway.

JESUS IS BETRAYED AND ARRESTED   Page **48**

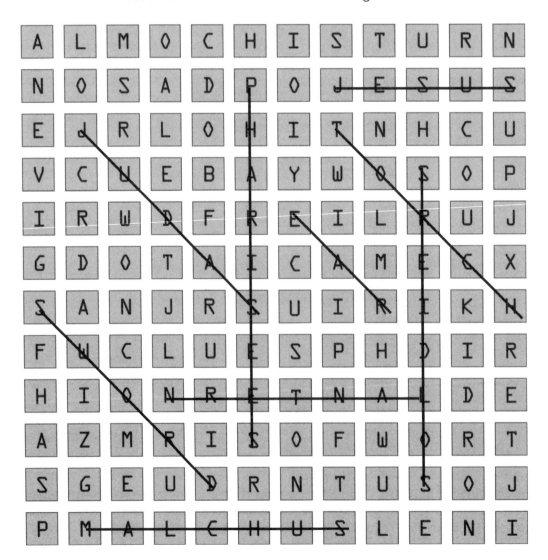

Now that you've met John
LOOK OUT FOR LUKE

AND MATTHEW AND MARK

Matthew
ISBN 1-85792-673-0
Mark
ISBN 1-85792-674-9
Luke
ISBN 1-85792-758-3
John
ISBN 1-85792-759-1

Good books with the real message of hope!

Christian Focus Publications publishes biblically-accurate books for adults and children. If you are looking for quality Bible teaching for children then we have a wide and excellent range of Bible story books - from board books to teenage fiction, we have it covered. You can also try our new Bible teaching Syllabus for 3-9 year olds and teaching materials for pre-school children.

These children's books are bright, fun and full of biblical truth, an ideal way to help children discover Jesus Christ for themselves. Our aim is to help children find out about God and get them enthusiastic about reading the Bible, now and later in their lives.

Find us at our web page: www.christianfocus.com